A Guide To Women's Mental Health Journey

SHE'S NOT

CRAZY

Stories Of Women Overcoming Mental Health Challenges And Dispelling Myths

DR LORRAINE BLALOCK

TABLE OF CONTENTS

INTRODUCTION

THE POWER OF WOMEN'S STORIES

The strength of the stories of women is in their capacity to dismantle the taboos and misinformation that often surround mental health issues. These are not only tales; they are a force for change and an example of the bravery, tenacity, and fortitude that women can muster while navigating the challenging terrain of their own mental health.

Women's experiences possess a special power to break the taboo that often develops mental health concerns. Through their narratives, they expose the challenges, anxieties, and victories they have faced on their travels. By doing this, they question the social conventions that have for too long supported stigma and silence. These tales provide a secure environment for candid discussions around mental health.

These stories aid in debunking myths and false beliefs that have aided in the ongoing misinformation about mental health issues. These ladies confront the prejudices and preconceptions that have stigmatized their lives by sharing their own narratives. Their disclosure of their realities offers a more realistic and empathetic representation of the intricacies involved in mental health.

These stories promote connection and empathy. They foster a feeling of humanity by putting readers in the shoes of persons who have struggled with mental health issues. The knowledge that they are not alone in their challenges may be a great consolation and source of hope for readers.

Inspiration may be found in the accounts of women who have faced their mental health issues head-on. These stories demonstrate the extraordinary fortitude and resiliency that may be mustered in the face of adversity. They show that with perseverance and support, rehabilitation and healing are not only feasible but also attainable.

Women's stories serve as a catalyst for change in addition to being a form of expression. They have the ability to change how society views and handles mental health. Women open the door for empathy, understanding, and optimism by sharing their story. These tales serve as a reminder that each person's path towards mental health is unique, and that by using storytelling to create a more compassionate and welcoming environment, we can celebrate the power of women's experiences and use them to pave the way for a better future.

CHAPTER ONE

SARAH'S TRIUMPH OVER ANXIETY

This chapter takes us on a journey with Sarah, a lady who has struggled with anxiety but has eventually overcome it. Sarah's tale demonstrates the fortitude and perseverance people may muster in the face of anxiety's sometimes crippling hold.

We use this chance to debunk some prevalent myths and misunderstandings about anxiety as we examine Sarah's story. We want to provide readers a more realistic knowledge of this intricate mental health issue by dispelling these falsehoods.

Sarah's path across the turbulent terrain of worry was a narrow one with many bends and twists. Her experience serves as a monument to the tenacity of the human spirit and a lesson that hope may exist even in the most hopeless circumstances.

Sarah had always performed much above average. She had a loving family, a successful job, and a close-knit group of friends who respected her self-assurance and grace. Beneath the surface of calmness and achievement, however, Sarah concealed a secret—a persistent enemy that she would eventually come to understand as worry.

It started slowly, like a little murmur on the periphery of her awareness. She first wrote it off as the usual stress of her hard work. She told herself that the restless nights, racing mind, and unwavering feeling of dread were just transient episodes. She assured herself she could take it; she was strong.

However, as the weeks passed and the months passed, that murmur in her head became louder and more persistent. Even the brightest of days seemed to be shadowed by a black cloud that seemed to be hovering above her. She was aware that something was wrong; this wasn't just stress; rather, it was anxiety, a phrase that could conjure feelings of bewilderment and terror.

Eliminating the misconception that anxiety was a sign of weakness was one of the hardest things Sarah had to do on her path. It was difficult for her to acknowledge that she was dealing with a mental health condition since she had always taken great pleasure in her strength and perseverance. It took her some time to realize that worry knew no bounds. Anybody might be impacted by it, regardless of their inner fortitude.

The notion that anxiousness would go away on its own was another lie she had to face. Not at all. It clung to her, a never-ending friend that appeared to feed off of her doubts and anxieties. She came to see that she couldn't defeat this evil on her alone and that she needed assistance.

Sarah struggled with the idea that her nervousness was only a product of her mind, something she could manage with pure will. Her body tensing in reaction to sometimes-irrational cues, her heart beating, she quickly realized it had psychological as well as physiological components.

One of the most damaging beliefs she came across was probably the idea that those who suffer from anxiety are only looking for attention. She was always reluctant to talk about her difficulties, and the stigma around mental illness only served to deepen her sense of loneliness. She fought a secret fight against anxiety, one that took place in the privacy of her own thoughts.

But Sarah wasn't alone. She set out on a path of comprehension, restoration, and recuperation under the direction of an empathetic therapist and with the help of her family. She engaged in mindfulness exercises, picked up coping mechanisms, and gradually started to reclaim her life.

We see Sarah's bravery and tenacity as we walk with her on her journey to overcome anxiety. Her experience serves as a potent reminder that anxiety is a struggle that has to be addressed, understood, and conquered rather than a sign of weakness. It's a tale of resilience and optimism that encourages people to look for assistance and support as they go through their own struggles with anxiety. Sarah's tale demonstrates that there is hope for a better, anxiety-free day ahead of us if we have access to the correct tools and assistance.

HIGHLIGHTS

Myth: *Anxiety is a sign of weakness.*

Reality: Anxiety is not a sign of weakness, but rather a common human response to stress and uncertainty. Sarah's journey highlights that even the strongest individuals can be affected by anxiety.

Myth: *Anxiety is just a passing feeling that will go away on its own.*

Reality: Anxiety can be a persistent and chronic condition for many individuals. Sarah's story underscores the importance of seeking help and support when anxiety becomes overwhelming.

Myth: *Anxiety is all in your head and can be easily controlled.*

Reality: Anxiety has both psychological and physiological components. It is not a matter of mere willpower or control. Sarah's experiences illustrate the complexities of managing anxiety.

Myth: *People with anxiety are just seeking attention.*

Reality: This myth perpetuates stigma and discourages open dialogue about mental health. Sarah's journey emphasizes the genuine struggle that individuals with anxiety face.

Through Sarah's story and the debunking of these myths, we aim to foster empathy, understanding, and support for those grappling with anxiety. Her triumph serves as an inspiration and a reminder that with the right resources and a support network, individuals can reclaim their lives from the clutches of anxiety. This chapter not only celebrates Sarah's resilience but also strives to dispel the myths that can hinder individuals from seeking the help and understanding they deserve.

CHAPTER TWO

MARIA'S BATTLE WITH DEPRESSION

We explore Maria's brave trek through the depths of despair in this chapter. Her narrative serves as both a sobering reminder that sadness knows no bounds and may affect even the most brilliant people, as well as a monument to the resiliency of the human spirit.

A young lady called Maria used to reside in a tiny yet lively town. For those who knew her, her laughter was like music, and her smile could lift the gloomiest of days. But nobody realized that Maria was secretly fighting despair, a powerful enemy. Maria's contagious laugh and bubbly demeanor had long been well-known. But those closest to her saw the brightness in her eyes progressively fade as her struggle with depression played out. It began with an unexplained melancholy that persisted way beyond life's typical ups and downs. She was caught in an unending circle of despair and thought that happiness was a thing of the past.

The idea that sadness is a sign of weakness was one of the illusions Maria had to deal with. She was by no means feeble. Her battle with depression really showed a great deal of courage and resiliency as she confronted a very strong opponent. The misconception that depression is just about feeling down has crept into both Maria's life and the thoughts of everyone who knew her. She thought her friends and family wouldn't understand, so she felt stuck in a web of silence and unable to talk to them about her troubles. Through her eyes, they saw the joyful, carefree Maria who was impervious to gloom.

One fallacy Maria came across was the notion that sadness was a transient emotional condition that would eventually go away. This false impression was dispelled by her experience, since despair was not a passing mood. It became an omnipresent, ominous fog that refused to go away. She also had to debunk the fallacy that depression was something that could be eliminated by mental adjustment. She realized that depression was more than just optimistic thinking; it was a complicated interaction of biological, psychological, and environmental elements.

One of the most destructive illusions she had to dispel was probably the idea that people who were depressed were just looking for attention. There is nothing that is more false than this. Maria yearned for comprehension, compassion, and sincere assistance instead of recognition for her hardships.

As the town came alive with activity one bright morning, Maria made the decision to face her inner demons. In an effort to debunk the misconceptions that had imprisoned her for so long, she started researching depression. She learned that depression was a complex web of feelings and physical symptoms, not simply a state of being down.

Maria's road of self-discovery and healing was paved with her understanding journey. She began talking to her loved ones about her difficulties, dispelling the stereotype that those who suffer from melancholy are helpless or attention-seekers. After being first taken aback by her disclosure, her family and friends showed her their love and support, understanding that sadness may strike anybody, regardless of looks.

She gained another crucial insight as she fought on: despair was not a reflection of her own shortcomings. She dispelled the illusion that she could just force herself to go through it or conquer it with determination. It was a multifaceted, intricate disease that needed time and expert assistance.

Maria started her road to recovery with the help of her family and a sympathetic therapist. They also dispelled the misconception that treatment was just for the helpless. She discovered that asking for assistance was not a sign of weakness but rather of strength and self-care.

Maria eventually regained control of her life because to her tenacity and the community's assistance. She debunked the idea that depression was a permanent condition. It could be a difficult and drawn-out struggle, but recovery was achievable.

Maria was seen as a ray of hope and understanding by the village that had known her as the always cheerful girl. She had not only overcome her depression but also debunked the stigma associated with it, raising awareness and providing compassion to others in need.

Maria's struggle with depression turned into a narrative of fortitude, development, and the ability to dispel the myths that sometimes surround mental health problems. She demonstrated how everyone, even the most outwardly happy people, may experience sadness and how much a friend or family's support can mean.

Maria went on to enjoy her life, her laughter being a true representation of her power and pleasure instead of a façade, and her tale inspired many people going through similar struggles.

We observe Maria's bravery and tenacity as we go with her through her depressive journey. Her experience serves as a powerful reminder that depression is a powerful enemy that requires care and therapy rather than a sign of weakness.

In addition to honoring Maria's tenacity, her inspiring tale aims to debunk the misconceptions that have helped to normalize depression. It is a request for understanding, empathy, and support for others who, like Maria, have struggled with this significant but sometimes unseen obstacle. Through her story, Maria sheds light on a route for rehabilitation and healing, one that gives individuals who struggle with depression hope for a better future.

HIGHLIGHTS

Myth: *Depression is a sign of weakness.*
Reality: Depression is not a sign of weakness. It is a complex mental health condition influenced by various factors, including genetics, brain chemistry, and life experiences. Maria's journey demonstrates her strength and resilience in facing this formidable adversary.

Myth: *Depression is just a temporary, fleeting feeling.*
Reality: Depression is not fleeting; it can persist for weeks, months, or even years. Maria's story dismantles the misconception that depression is a passing emotion and underscores the chronic nature of the condition.

Myth: *You can will away depression with a change of mindset.*
Reality: Depression is not something that can be overcome through positive thinking alone. It involves complex biological and psychological processes.

Maria's experience shows that it is not a matter of willpower but a condition that demands appropriate treatment.

Myth: *People with depression are seeking attention.*
Reality: Those battling depression are not seeking attention; they are seeking understanding, empathy, and support. Maria's story highlights the deep need for compassion and genuine support when dealing with depression.

By dispelling these myths and shedding light on the realities of depression through Maria's journey, this chapter aims to foster empathy and provide a more accurate understanding of this complex mental health challenge. It encourages readers to approach depression with compassion and to support those who may be enduring this invisible battle. Maria's story serves as a beacon of hope, illustrating that recovery

is possible when met with understanding
and the right resources.

CHAPTER THREE

EMILY'S JOURNEY THROUGH POSTPARTUM DEPRESSION

We follow Emily as she navigates the difficult terrain of postpartum depression in this chapter. Her experience serves as a tribute to the bravery and perseverance needed to deal with the difficult emotions that often accompany delivery.

Like many new moms, Emily had anticipated the happiness and pleasure that come with having a baby. But instead, she faced an unanticipated foe: postpartum depression. Her struggle with this illness dispelled many of the misconceptions that surround it.

Emily's life has been filled with experiences, from traveling to far-off places to succeeding in the business world. Her brilliant smile, inexhaustible energy, and courageous personality were well-known qualities about her. She was excited about starting a new journey when she learned she was going to become a mother. She felt ready for the voyage that would change her life since she had read every book and taken the parenting workshops.

Emily's life completely collapsed at the birth of her daughter Lily. While Emily accepted that tiredness, insomnia, and the never-ending responsibilities of motherhood were all a part of the experience, she immediately sensed that there was something more, something that felt oppressive and heavy.

She dismissed it at first, blaming the drastic changes in her life for her enduring melancholy and debilitating anxiety. Though everyone assured her that feeling overwhelmed was common after giving birth, Emily was unable to resist the pall of hopelessness that loomed over her as the days stretched into weeks. It went beyond the "baby blues." It was something more profound that she was unable to overcome.

The idea that postpartum depression was an indication of inadequate mothering was the first misconception Emily encountered on her path through the condition. It seemed as if the one thing she had spent her whole life preparing for was failing her. Emily's resilience surfaced when she accepted that she was not to blame for her postpartum depression and that seeking assistance was a brave act rather than a sign of weakness.

The idea that postpartum depression will go as soon as it appeared was another fallacy. Emily's experience demonstrated that it was a chronic, all-encompassing illness that needed patience and attention to heal. Her experience helped her realize that postpartum depression was a serious threat to her mental health rather than a passing mood.

Emily also came across the fallacy that by concentrating only on her child, she might overcome postpartum depression. It didn't take her long to understand that she couldn't win this war by herself or by pure willpower. She required comprehension, assistance, and, in her instance, medical attention.

Emily had a very difficult time busting the stereotype that moms suffering from postpartum depression were abusing or neglecting their infants. She really did love Lily more than anything in the world, but the sadness made it difficult for her to truly appreciate being a mother. It was a serious internal conflict, not carelessness.

Emily's bravery and tenacity are on display as we accompany her on her road through postpartum depression. She took on the myths and false beliefs about this illness head-on and came out looking strong and resilient. Her experience gives hope and the knowledge that postpartum depression can be overcome with the correct tools and assistance to anyone who may find themselves on a similar journey.

Emily's experience with postpartum depression served as evidence that even the most courageous people can overcome the most difficult obstacles, and that they may rise from the shadows into the light of hope and healing when given the appropriate support and understanding.

HIGHLIGHTS

Myth: *Postpartum depression is a sign of inadequacy.*

Reality: Postpartum depression is not a reflection of a mother's inadequacy. It is a legitimate medical condition caused by a combination of hormonal, emotional, and environmental factors. Emily's story illustrates her strength as she faced this challenge head-on.

Myth: *Postpartum depression is a short-lived "baby blues."*

Reality: Postpartum depression is not synonymous with the common "baby blues." It is a distinct and more prolonged condition, often persisting for weeks or months. Emily's experience dispels the myth that it is a brief and fleeting emotional state.

Myth: *A new mother can overcome postpartum depression by simply focusing on her baby.*

Reality: Postpartum depression is not something that can be willed away by redirecting one's focus. It requires understanding, support, and often professional treatment. Emily's story underscores the need for comprehensive care and emotional support during this challenging time.

Myth: *Mothers with postpartum depression are neglecting or harming their babies.*

Reality: Mothers with postpartum depression are not neglectful or harmful. They are grappling with a serious mental health issue. Emily's journey emphasizes that these mothers need understanding, compassion, and appropriate care.

Through Emily's story, this chapter seeks to dispel the myths that have contributed to the stigma surrounding postpartum depression. It highlights the importance of acknowledging this condition as a real and valid experience that can affect any new mother. The chapter aims to encourage empathy and support for those facing postpartum depression, emphasizing that recovery is possible with the right resources and understanding. Emily's story offers hope and a path toward healing for mothers navigating this challenging terrain.

CHAPTER FOUR

LISA'S RESILIENCE IN THE FACE OF TRAUMA

Lisa was a lady who lived in a quiet community. Her unshakable friendliness, caring personality, and warm smile were well-known qualities about her. Lisa was the center of her neighborhood, always willing to provide support or a listening ear. Lisa seemed happy on the outside, but she was hiding a deep trauma that had followed her for years.

There have been tremendous highs and heartbreaking lows in Lisa's life. She had overcome obstacles that would have shattered most people, yet she persevered with an incredible fortitude that would inspire respect in anybody.

A horrific incident that deeply damaged Lisa's mental health was one of the turning points in her life. Although she had survived the tragedy, the misunderstandings and myths around it often made her suffering worse.

Lisa's parents died in a horrific accident many years ago, and she was the only one who survived. Her heart and intellect were deeply scarred by the horrible incident. Her nighttime sleep was difficult, and she often woke up from intense dreams about the catastrophe. Overwhelming anxiousness and bothersome thoughts dominated her days. The event had the potential to cast a shadow over her life.

However, Lisa was certain that her past would not dictate her future. She defied the stereotype that going to therapy was a sign of weakness by getting professional assistance. Her therapist gave her a secure environment in which to face her suffering and develop coping skills. Through her treatment, Lisa came to understand that addressing her trauma head-on with bravery was what resilience was all about, not forgetting or avoiding it.

There were many highs and lows on her path to resilience. There were times when she felt like giving up because of how heavy her background was. However, Lisa found strength in her friends, her network of support, and her unyielding will to recover.

She threw herself into volunteering and drawing, things that made her happy. She turned her suffering into art and found comfort in serving others. She dispelled the misconception that trauma could only result in hopelessness by demonstrating that recovery and development were also viable results.

Lisa started to exhibit resilience in her day-to-day activities. She stopped letting her painful past define who she was.

Rather, she found courage in them, inspiring herself to live life to the fullest and pay tribute to her parents.

Over time, Lisa had fewer nightmares and increased control over her anxieties. Despite the fact that she was aware that trauma recovery was not a straight line, she saw growth and self-compassion along the way. She demolished the illusion that healing needed to happen quickly and completely.

Her tale of tenacity started to inspire those around her. Lisa dispelled the misconception that trauma should be hidden by being transparent about her experiences. Her openness served as a bridge, letting people know they weren't alone in their troubles and that it was OK to ask for assistance.

Lisa persevered throughout the years, demonstrating that resilience meant more than simply overcoming hardship—it also meant emerging from it stronger. She demonstrated to her community that healing was achievable with bravery, support, and self-compassion, and that a horrific past did not have to dictate one's future.

Lisa's journey served as a monument to the strength of resiliency and a poignant reminder that the human spirit is capable of rising above unspeakable suffering and emerging stronger than before. Her experience dispelled many of the stereotypes surrounding trauma and the healing process and became a source of hope for people navigating their own journeys toward resilience and recovery.

HIGHLIGHTS

Myth: *People who experience trauma are weak.*

Reality: Lisa's strength was evident in her ability to endure and survive trauma. It took immense courage to confront the scars it left behind, and it was not a sign of weakness but of her indomitable spirit.

Myth: *Trauma is something that can be easily forgotten or overcome.*

Reality: Trauma is not something that can be easily forgotten or overcome. It leaves a lasting impact on an individual's mental and emotional well-being. Lisa's story dispels the myth that trauma can be erased with time or willpower.

Myth: *Talking about trauma will only make it worse.*

Reality: Talking about trauma in a safe and supportive environment is often a crucial part of the healing process. Lisa's resilience lay in her ability to confront her past and seek the help she needed.

Myth: *Trauma survivors are damaged beyond repair.*
Reality: Trauma survivors are not beyond repair. Lisa's story is a testament to the fact that with resilience, support, and the right resources, individuals can find a path to healing and recovery.

As we delve into Lisa's remarkable journey through trauma, we witness her courage, her resilience, and her ability to dispel the myths that have often perpetuated the stigma surrounding this challenging experience. Her story is an inspiration to all who face trauma, showing that recovery and resilience are possible, even in the face of the most harrowing circumstances.

CHAPTER FIVE

OLIVIA'S STRUGGLE WITH EATING DISORDERS

There was a young lady called Olivia who lived in a little town. Olivia was a gifted and intelligent painter who was well-known for her charming compositions and kind nature. But Olivia was concealing a terrible secret under her colorful exterior: she was struggling with an eating issue.

There were many myths and misunderstandings concerning eating disorders in the community. Some assumed eating disorders were merely a phase that teens went through, while others thought that only females who had poor self-esteem battled with these kinds of problems. Olivia was eager to debunk these fallacies since she knew better.

Olivia had started her eating problem journey when she was a teenager. Her drive to fit in, pressure from school, and society beauty standards had gradually worn her down. She started limiting her food consumption because she thought that having control over her diet would help her feel more in charge of her life. She was becoming more and more alone in her fight with anorexia, which was separating her from her friends and family.

Olivia came to the realization one day that she had to turn away from this harmful course. She sought advice from a therapist who specialized in eating problems since she realized she needed treatment. She began her road to recovery with their help.

Olivia discovered early on in her path that the misconceptions about eating disorders were untrue. She was not the average low-self-esteem "skinny" girl. Actually, anybody may be impacted by eating disorders, regardless of their looks or level of confidence. Olivia served as real-life evidence that eating disorders might affect anybody.

Olivia discovered throughout her treatment sessions that eating problems were not only passing stages. These were complicated mental health problems that needed guidance, comprehension, and assistance from professionals. Olivia was committed to educating her community and dispelling the myths associated with eating disorders.

She began by candidly telling her friends and family about her experience. Olivia described the everyday challenges, crippling worry, and warped sense of self that accompanied her illness. She also underlined that asking for assistance was a show of strength rather than weakness.

Those around Olivia were greatly impacted by her candor. Her family and friends started to see that eating disorders were more than simply a desire to be skinny and started to accept the truth of it. Olivia's narrative encouraged her family members to be more understanding, kind, and knowledgeable.

Olivia's fight with her eating issue started to show results over time. She kept painting, transferring her feelings onto the canvas and finding comfort in her creations. Her artistic endeavors began to mirror her recuperation process, striking a chord with others going through similar struggles.

Olivia expanded her following via public speaking engagements and art shows. By sharing her experience and promoting understanding and compassion, she debunked the misconceptions associated with eating disorders. She contributed to the understanding in her community that eating disorders were common, intricate, and could impact anybody.

Olivia's story served as a monument to her tenacity and her dedication to debunking the myths associated with eating disorders. She not only got her life back, but she also turned into a ray of hope for those facing comparable challenges. She was rewriting the story of eating disorders with every painting and speech she gave, demonstrating that they were something that could be addressed, overcome, and triumphed over with support from loved ones and medical professionals.

Olivia's tale served as a poignant reminder that courage can always be found in adversity, and that truth may always be lying in wait to be discovered beneath myths. She was a young lady who had experienced a severe battle throughout her life, one that was hidden from view. Her struggle with eating disorders had put her fortitude and tenacity to the test, but it had also highlighted the falsehoods and misunderstandings that often accompany this difficult mental health issue.

HIGHLIGHTS

Myth: *Eating disorders are solely about vanity.*

Reality: Olivia's experience illustrates that eating disorders are not just about vanity or the desire to look a certain way. They often stem from deeper emotional and psychological issues that demand understanding and compassion.

Myth: *Eating disorders are a choice.*

Reality: Olivia's battle revealed that eating disorders are not a choice but a serious mental health condition. They can be incredibly isolating and destructive, making it imperative to approach them with empathy and support rather than judgment.

Myth: *You can simply eat your way out of an eating disorder.*

Reality: Olivia's story dispels the myth that individuals with eating disorders can simply "eat their way out" of the condition. It is a complex struggle involving psychological, emotional, and physical aspects, often requiring professional help and support.

Myth: *Eating disorders only affect young women.*
Reality: Eating disorders can affect individuals of any age, gender, or background. Olivia's journey shows that it's crucial to dispel the stereotype that they exclusively impact young women and to promote a more inclusive understanding of this condition.

We see Olivia's tenacity and her capacity to dispel the misunderstandings around this mental health issue as we follow her through her fight with eating disorders. Her experience serves as a reminder that eating disorders have many facets and that, with the correct help, awareness, and resources, recovery is achievable. Olivia's story debunks misconceptions about eating disorders and provides a way forward for others to seek support in order to overcome the stigma associated with eating disorders.

CHAPTER SIX

AVA'S LIFE WITH BIPOLAR DISORDER

Ava was well-known for having a vibrant personality, an endless supply of energy, and the capacity to brighten every space she walked into. Beneath the colorful appearance, however, was a secret struggle with bipolar illness, a disease that would challenge the beliefs and preconceptions surrounding this mental health issue while also setting her on a turbulent path of self-discovery and perseverance.

When Ava was in her late teens, she was diagnosed with bipolar illness. Her path was filled with highs and lows. Although having bipolar illness was a difficult mental health condition to live with, Ava was determined to overcome the stigma and misunderstandings around the disease.

The idea that bipolar illness is only about mood swings is one of the most pervasive fallacies about it. It was a common misconception that people with bipolar illness were unable to regulate their emotions and might swing in a matter of minutes from severe highs to terrible lows. Ava was aware that debunking this notion was necessary.

Ava had a far more complex experience with bipolar illness. She clarified that there were several stages, each lasting a few weeks or even months, such as manic periods and depressed spells. She would have sudden spurts of confidence, vitality, and inventiveness during manic episodes, but sometimes these would develop into dangerous actions. Conversely, depressive episodes bring with them a crippling sensation of despair and melancholy.

Notwithstanding the falsehoods propagated about her illness, Ava was resolved to take charge of her life. She looked for both medicine and treatment to help control her bipolar condition. Her therapist helped her understand her disease and how to deal with its obstacles in addition to being a source of support.

With the help of her therapist, Ava discovered that bipolar illness was a real medical disease that was often caused by chemical imbalances in the brain, not a decision or a sign of weakness. She helped her community recognize that, with the correct assistance, persons with bipolar illness could have successful lives, by emphasizing the need of treatment and management.

Ava was also committed to dispelling the myth that those who suffer from bipolar illness are unstable or incapable of working. She had a prosperous career in the arts, often flourishing when she went through manic episodes and her imagination ran wild. She channeled her energy constructively by showcasing her artwork and used it as a vehicle for expressing her feelings.

Through her public speaking engagements and art exhibits, Ava told the tale of her battle with bipolar disease. She de-stigmatized the concept of getting assistance for mental health difficulties by being transparent about her medicines and course of treatment. Her message was quite clear: getting medical attention wasn't a show of weakness, but of power.

The community found inspiration in Ava's path. She busted the misconceptions that bipolar illness was incurable or that it characterized a person's lifelong condition. Rather, she emphasized that people with bipolar disorder could manage their illness and have happy, fulfilled lives if they received the appropriate care, counseling, and medication.

Ava persevered on her quest with dignity and fortitude as the years went by. She was a beacon of hope for those facing comparable difficulties as well as proof that bipolar illness could be controlled. One narrative and one brushstroke at a time, she dispelled the myths, demonstrating that recovery from bipolar disease was not only feasible but totally attainable. Ava's life served as a real-life illustration of how truth and resiliency may exist behind any myth and wait to be revealed.

HIGHLIGHTS

Myth: *Bipolar disorder is simply mood swings.*

Reality: Ava's story highlights that bipolar disorder is not merely mood swings. It is a complex mental health condition characterized by significant shifts in mood, energy, and behavior. It's not something that can be casually equated to everyday fluctuations in emotions.

Myth: *People with bipolar disorder can control their mood swings with willpower.*

Reality: Ava's journey through bipolar disorder underscores the fact that this condition cannot be controlled through sheer willpower. It is a medical condition influenced by neurological factors, and individuals often need treatment and support to manage it effectively.

Myth: *Bipolar disorder is a lifelong sentence to instability.*

Reality: Ava's experience shows that while bipolar disorder is a lifelong condition, it is not an unchangeable sentence to instability. With proper treatment, support, and resilience, individuals with bipolar disorder can lead fulfilling lives and achieve stability.

Myth: *People with bipolar disorder are always in extreme manic or depressive states.*

Reality: Bipolar disorder is not always about extreme states. There can be periods of stability, and it varies among individuals. Ava's story emphasizes the need to dispel the misconception that those with bipolar disorder are perpetually in extreme states of mania or depression.

Joining Ava on her journey to overcome bipolar disorder, we see her bravery, tenacity, and capacity to debunk the beliefs that often contribute to the stigma associated with this illness. Her experience offers hope and a way back to recovery to anyone struggling with bipolar disease. It highlights that people with bipolar illness may have stable and productive lives and that recovery is achievable with the correct tools, knowledge, and assistance. Ava's narrative serves as a tribute to the resilience of the human spirit and the significance of dispelling the stereotypes associated with mental health conditions like bipolar illness.

CHAPTER SEVEN

HARLEY'S RECOVERY FROM SELF-HARM

A young lady called Harley lived in a quiet suburban area. Harley was well-known for her quick wit, brilliant smile, and compassionate demeanor, but she also battled self-harm, a deeply concealed secret, beneath her happy exterior. Along the way, her path to rehabilitation will expose the misconceptions and myths surrounding self-harm in addition to healing her own wounds. Harley's narrative is one of tenacity, optimism, and the road to healing after a covert struggle with self-harm.

The idea that self-harming is just an attention-seeking habit is one of the most widespread misconceptions regarding it. It was a common belief that those who self-harmed were either seeking sympathy or attempting to control other people. Harley was well aware of how untrue this was.

In her adolescent years, Harley began self-harming as a coping mechanism for intense feelings, tension, and inner conflict. When life appeared out of control, it was her method of regaining control. She came to comprehend that self-harm was not an attention-seeking behavior, but rather a dysfunctional coping technique for emotional suffering.

When Harley realized she had to get treatment from a therapist who specialized in self-harm and self-destructive tendencies, she realized she couldn't go on down this risky road. She started her road to recovery with the help of her loved ones and the direction of her therapist.

Harley developed more constructive coping mechanisms and the underlying reasons of her self-harming habits throughout her treatment sessions. She understood that self-harm was not a deception technique, but rather an indication of mental suffering and a cry for assistance. Her progress was steady but sluggish, and she was committed to ending the self-harm cycle.

Harley's road to recovery served as evidence of her fortitude and resiliency. She made the decision to candidly tell her tale to her close friends and relatives. She described the severe emotional suffering that drove her to self-harm, stressing that it was an indication of severe misery rather than a cry for help.

While pursuing her rehabilitation and recuperation, Harley also debunked the stereotype that only adolescents participated in self-harming behaviors. She revealed that self-harm was not exclusive to any one group, as it may impact individuals of different ages and socioeconomic backgrounds.

People in Harley's vicinity were more understanding and sympathetic after hearing her tale. Her loved ones understood that self-harm was not something she could readily manage, and they gave her the unconditional support she needed.

Harley's story served as a real-life illustration that self-harm healing was achievable. She kept up her treatment, developed better coping strategies, and discovered more useful techniques for controlling her emotions. By telling her experience and highlighting the fact that asking for assistance is a show of strength rather than weakness, she shattered the misconceptions associated with self-harm.

Harley's life changed throughout time from one of self-destruction to one of recovery and development. Her narrative not only aided in her recovery but also demonstrated to her neighborhood that any adversity could be overcome with courage and optimism. Harley demonstrated that self-harm was a complicated problem requiring knowledge, empathy, and expert assistance. She dispelled the myths and prejudices around self-harm by her bravery, demonstrating that anybody who aspired to recovery and healing could find them.

HIGHLIGHTS

Myth: *Self-harm is just a cry for attention.*

Reality: Harley's journey demonstrates that self-harm is not merely a cry for attention. It is a deeply ingrained coping mechanism that individuals use to manage emotional pain and distress. It is not a choice but a sign of inner turmoil.

Myth: *People who self-harm can stop at any time if they want to.*

Reality: Harley's experience dispels the myth that self-harm is a behavior that can be stopped at will. It often becomes an addictive and entrenched pattern that requires understanding, support, and professional help to overcome.

Myth: *Self-harm is a sign of being mentally unstable.*

Reality: Harley's story challenges the misconception that self-harm is a sign of mental instability. It is often a response to emotional distress and does not define a person's overall mental health. Recovery is possible, and individuals can regain stability.

Myth: *Self-harm is always about seeking suicide.*
Reality: Self-harm is not always linked to suicidal intentions. Harley's story emphasizes that it is a coping mechanism used to deal with emotional pain, but it does not necessarily indicate a desire to end one's life.

Harley's story serves as an inspiration for those grappling with self-harm, offering hope and a path toward healing. Her experience underscores that recovery is possible with the right resources, understanding, and support. It encourages individuals who are struggling with self-harm to seek help and challenges society to provide a compassionate and empathetic environment for those on their journey towards healing. Self-harm is not a

simple issue, and Harley's triumph
shows that with resilience and support, it
can be overcome.

CHAPTER EIGHT

EMMA'S JOURNEY FROM ISOLATION TO CONNECTION

Although Emma had always been recognized for her brilliance and inventiveness, she had felt alone and cut off from society for the most of her life. Her transformation from loneliness to connection served as a counterbalance to the stereotypes associated with loneliness and isolation, as well as a monument to her resilience.

Emma had been fighting social anxiety for years, like an unseen enemy. She often felt as if she didn't belong and was an outsider. She dreaded social events and large groups. The mere notion of striking up a conversation or entering a crowded environment was intimidating.

One of the most widespread misconceptions regarding isolation was that people like Emma chose to be alone or were antisocial. Emma was aware that this notion was untrue, however. Her severe social anxiety prevented her from interacting with others, despite her deep need for connection, which contributed to her isolation.

For years, Emma's worry had kept her apart, keeping her from pursuing her goals and building deep connections. She made the decision to seek assistance from a therapist who specializes in anxiety problems since she felt she couldn't go on living alone.

Under the direction of her therapist, Emma started her quest to conquer social anxiety. She gained the ability to face her concerns and question her negative thinking patterns. She began to put herself out there gradually, participating in group activities and establishing relationships with others who had similar interests to hers.

With the aid of her newly formed friends and her treatment, Emma started to debunk the notion that loneliness was a decision. She described her seclusion as an enforced captivity from which she yearned to escape. She stressed that fighting against the unrelenting hold of dread and anxiety was more important to many people like her than desiring to be alone themselves.

Emma's narrative encouraged empathy and understanding in her society. After learning about her difficulties, her friends were patient and encouraging in helping her on her path to connection. They came to see that helping others who battled with isolation was a gesture of love and compassion, and that isolation was not necessarily a decision.

Emma found that loneliness was not exclusive to introverts or those suffering from social anxiety as she persisted on her journey towards establishing connections. She dispelled the misconception that loneliness and isolation were limited to a certain set of people by meeting individuals from all walks of life who had felt alienated at some time.

Emma's experience served as a real-life example of how people may connect, even after feeling alone for a long time. She conquered her social anxieties, made true friends, and started participating in things that didn't seem conceivable. Her experience demonstrated to her community that getting treatment is a crucial first step in addressing mental health disorders, which may be the cause of isolation.

Emma changed over time from someone who felt stuck in isolation to someone who lived on interpersonal relationships. In addition to assisting her in healing, her experience dispelled stereotypes about loneliness by demonstrating that everyone can find a way to connect and feel like they belong, whatever their upbringing or challenges. Emma's bravery and tenacity demolished the misconceptions about loneliness and offered hope to others who yearned for a feeling of belonging.

HIGHLIGHTS

Myth: *Social anxiety is just shyness.*

Reality: Emma's story illustrates that social anxiety is not merely shyness. It is an intense fear of social situations and the potential for negative judgment. It can be debilitating, often preventing individuals from engaging in social activities they desire.

Myth: *People with social anxiety just need to "get over it."*

Reality: Emma's journey dispels the myth that people with social anxiety can simply "get over it" by pushing themselves into social situations. It is a complex condition that often requires a combination of self-compassion, therapy, and gradual exposure to overcome.

Myth: *Isolation is a choice for people with social anxiety.*

Reality: Emma's story underscores that isolation is not a choice for those with social anxiety. It is a coping mechanism to manage the overwhelming anxiety and fear. Recovery involves breaking free from this pattern.

Myth: *Social anxiety is something that can't be changed.*
Reality: Emma's experience challenges the misconception that social anxiety is a permanent state. With the right support and resources, individuals with social anxiety can learn to manage their condition and cultivate meaningful connections.

Emma's path is one of bravery, resiliency, and the capacity to dispel beliefs that support the stigma associated with social anxiety and solitude. Her experience offers hope and a way to healing and connection to others who are struggling with social anxiety.

CHAPTER NINE

ISABELLA'S VICTORY OVER PTSD

She had endured hardships from an early age that would have shattered many, yet she had an unbreakable spirit. But the struggle that raged within her own head was the most difficult one she had to fight: Post-Traumatic Stress Disorder (PTSD). Her name was Isabella.

Isabella's life has been characterized by terrifying recollections of suffering as well as extraordinary bravery. Her battle with Post-Traumatic Stress Disorder (PTSD) would put her courage, fortitude, and capacity to dispel the myths and false beliefs that sometimes accompany this difficult mental health issue to the test.

She had always been a fighter, taking on the challenges of life head-on. But a very traumatic experience left her with wounds that compromised her mental and emotional health. Her road to healing began with dispelling the misconceptions and lies surrounding PTSD.

She hardly ever discussed the event that had set off her post-traumatic stress disorder. She was emotionally damaged by the incident from her past and was plagued by strong recollections of it. She made an effort for years to bury, suppress, and hide those memories. However, they continued to surface like an unrelenting storm, giving her anxiety, panic attacks, and restless nights.

Isabella's first step toward success was admitting she was in need of assistance. She went in search of a therapist, someone who might help her navigate the perilous path of her memories. It was not simple. It was a difficult and painful process to relive the trauma, face the ghosts of the past, and open old wounds. However, Isabella saw a ray of hope and a light at the end of a very long tunnel with each treatment session.

The idea that PTSD is incurable is among the most common misconceptions about it. Isabella was going to disprove this. She dutifully went to therapy, practiced grounding, and gained control over her triggers. When she joined support groups and met others who had battled comparable demons, she also learned about the value of them. Isabella gained new strength from the coping mechanisms and tales they shared.

Isabella started to take control of her life gradually but steadily. She picked up painting again, something she had put down at the lowest points of her PTSD. Her use of art as a means of emotional expression and pain management evolved into a kind of therapy unto itself.

Her canvas's vibrant hues reflected the brightness that was coming back into her life.

Myth number two about PTSD is that it is a lifelong condition. Isabella understood that although she couldn't alter the past, she could control the future. She concentrated on establishing objectives and creating a better future while she proceeded with her recuperation. She formed new connections and revived old ones, surrounding herself with encouraging people.

Isabella's triumph over all of this was not just her own; it was evidence of the human spirit's tenacity. She demonstrated that even the most severe mental health issues could be resolved with the correct care, a solid support network, and persistent willpower.

Despite the ups and downs, failures and victories along the way, Isabella refused to let her past determine her future. She had broken the illusion that PTSD had the last word in her life and taken it back. Isabella's triumph served as a ray of hope for anybody struggling with their own history, showing them that, with bravery and perseverance, they too might discover the end of the dark tunnel.

HIGHLIGHTS

Myth: *PTSD is a sign of weakness.*
Reality: Isabella's story demonstrated that PTSD is not a sign of weakness. It can affect even the strongest individuals when faced with overwhelming traumatic experiences. Her journey illustrated that seeking help is a courageous act, not a sign of inadequacy.

Myth: *PTSD is a condition that only affects military veterans.*
Reality: Isabella's experience dispelled the myth that PTSD is exclusive to military veterans. It can affect anyone who has experienced trauma. Her story highlighted the importance of recognizing the broader impact of PTSD on individuals from various backgrounds.

Myth: *People with PTSD should just "move on."*
Reality: Isabella's journey highlighted that individuals with PTSD cannot

simply "move on." It is a complex mental health condition that requires treatment, understanding, and support to heal from the profound impact of trauma.

Myth: *People with PTSD are forever trapped in their trauma.*
Reality: Isabella's story challenged the misconception that individuals with PTSD are trapped in their trauma forever. With resilience, the right resources, and the support of loved ones, they can learn to manage and, in some cases, overcome the symptoms of PTSD.

We followed Isabella on her quest to overcome PTSD, and we saw her bravery, resiliency, and capacity to debunk the falsehoods that have helped to normalize this difficult illness. Her experience offered hope and a pathEsse to recovery to those struggling with PTSD, inspiring them.

Isabella's story demonstrated the transformational potential of healing. Her story demonstrated how people might overcome PTSD and come out from under the shadow of trauma if they had the necessary resources, support, and perseverance. Her experience served as a monument to the resilience of the human spirit and its capacity to rise above even the most trying circumstances.

CHAPTER TEN

SOFIA'S STRUGGLE WITH SUBSTANCE ABUSE

Sofia's life had been a rollercoaster of highs and lows, marked by a silent battle that had been consuming her from within. Her journey through substance abuse was one that would test her strength, her resilience, and her ability to challenge the myths and misconceptions surrounding this complex mental health challenge.

Sofia had always been a vivacious and adventurous spirit. She had a taste for excitement, but over time, that love for adventure led her down a treacherous path of addiction.

Sofia's story was not always one of despair. She was a bright and ambitious individual, with dreams of a promising future. Her journey into substance abuse began as a misguided attempt to cope with the stress and pressures of her demanding job and personal life. At first, it seemed like a temporary escape, a way to forget her problems and relax.

But what began as an occasional indulgence soon evolved into a habit, and before she knew it, it had taken control of her life. She found herself trapped in a vicious cycle of dependence, using substances to numb her emotions, only to wake up each day with a heavier burden.

Sofia's struggle was marked by isolation. She withdrew from her friends and family, feeling ashamed of her addiction. She thought she could handle it on her own, but it was a battle she was losing with every passing day. She would often look at her reflection in the mirror, wondering where the vibrant and hopeful person she once was had gone.

The first step in her journey was to confront the myths that often surround substance abuse. One of the most significant myths surrounding substance abuse is the idea that it's a choice or a sign of weakness. Sofia knew firsthand the overpowering grip addiction had on her life. It was not a choice but a relentless force that she was desperate to break free from.

Sofia's turning point came when she reached out to a therapist who specialized in addiction recovery. It was a small yet monumental step towards reclaiming her life. In therapy, she confronted the root causes of her addiction, delving into the emotional pain and trauma she had been trying to escape.

With the support of her therapist and a newfound determination, Sofia slowly began her journey of recovery. She attended support group meetings where she met others who had walked the same path. Hearing their stories and sharing her own struggles brought a sense of connection and hope.

Recovery was far from easy. There were relapses and moments of doubt, but Sofia never gave up. She had shattered the myth that substance abuse was insurmountable. Each day of sobriety became a small victory, a step towards regaining her life.

As Sofia's journey continued, she realized that she was not defined by her past mistakes. Her strength and resilience had been tested, and she had emerged from the shadows of addiction as a stronger person. She rebuilt her relationships, rekindled her passions, and discovered a new purpose - to help others facing similar struggles.

Sofia's story was a testament to the power of recovery and the importance of breaking the stigma surrounding substance abuse. She proved that addiction was not a life sentence but a battle that could be won with the right support and determination. Sofia's struggle had transformed into a story of resilience, hope, and a brighter future.

HIGHLIGHTS

Myth: *Substance abuse is a choice.*
Reality: Sofia's story illustrated that substance abuse is not a simple choice. It is a complex condition influenced by biological, psychological, and environmental factors. Her experience revealed that it was not a matter of willpower but a deep-seated struggle.

Myth: *People who abuse substances are morally flawed.*
Reality: Sofia's journey dispelled the myth that people who struggle with substance abuse are morally flawed. It's a condition that transcends moral judgments and often requires empathy and support to overcome.

Myth: *Substance abuse is a sign of weakness.*
Reality: Sofia's experience highlighted that substance abuse is not a sign of weakness but a genuine challenge that individuals face. Her journey showcased

the strength and resilience that can emerge when confronting this struggle.

Myth: *People with substance abuse issues are beyond help.*
Reality: Sofia's story challenged the misconception that those with substance abuse issues are beyond help. With the right resources, understanding, and support, recovery is possible, and individuals can find their way back to a fulfilling life.

As we joined Sofia on her journey through substance abuse, we witnessed her courage and resilience, and her ability to challenge the myths that often perpetuated the stigma surrounding this condition. Her story served as an inspiration for those grappling with substance abuse, offering hope and a path toward healing.

Sofia's experience underscored the transformative power of recovery. Her journey showed that with resilience, the right support, and the right resources, individuals could overcome even the darkest of challenges. Her story was a testament to the strength of the human spirit and its ability to find the way to healing and triumph over substance abuse.

A MESSAGE OF HOPE

To all the remarkable women navigating the often challenging path of mental health, I want to send a message of hope and solidarity. Each of you is an embodiment of strength and resilience, even on the toughest days.

Dealing with mental health challenges can be a daunting journey, but it's essential to recognize that seeking help and support is an act of courage, not a sign of weakness. Your ability to confront these difficulties head-on is a testament to your inner power.

It's important to acknowledge that mental health struggles are not solitary battles. You are part of a community of women who have faced similar challenges, and your experiences can be a source of support and connection. Together, we can break down the stigma surrounding mental health and foster an environment of understanding and empathy.

While the road ahead may seem uncertain, remember that there are brighter days awaiting you. Your journey is unique, and your resilience is inspiring. Embrace the moments of triumph, no matter how small, and reach out to the people who care about your well-being. You are never alone in this journey.

Hold onto hope, practice self-compassion, and keep believing in your own strength. Your story is a beacon of light for others facing similar struggles, and your determination will pave the way for a better tomorrow.